Yeshua's Dog
A Gospel Love Story

by Barbara Rogers
Illustrated by Tamaris Johnson

For Reverend
Susan Campbell Church

Yeshua's Dog: A Gospel Love Story
Copyright © 2011 by Barbara Rogers
ISBN 978-0-9834956-0-4
All rights reserved

SpiritBooks
wilson@spiritbooks.me

For more information: www.spiritbooks.me

Printed in the United States by LightningSource

1.Jesus; 2. Gospel 3. Holy Land; 4. Bible; 5. Dog Devotion;
6. Dog Inspiration; 7. Dog Stories

ISBN 978-0-9834956-0-4
Library of Congress Control Number
Manufactured in the United States of America

Cover design and interior illustrations by Tamaris Johnson
For prints of illustrations contact tamaris39@gmail.com

First Edition 2011

A Note on Names

Yeshua is the name Jesus would have been known by in New Testament times. It is pronounced Yeh-shu'-a. Cherem is pronounced Khe-rem' and means "the selfless one."

Table of Contents

River Jordan — Baptist

Chapter One

Stirrings

The rocky Galilean hills glowed red in the early morning sunlight. Above them, streaks of gray cloud faded into the blue sky and disappeared. It would be another day without rain, and water would be hard to find if you were an animal on his own. A golden-brown dog, like so many others in ancient Palestine, stopped on a dusty road to lick his knee. He had to sit down and twist around to do it, and the effort tired him.

The dog was so thin his ribs stuck out. His kneecap pointed sideways. It had never been the same since his old owner had kicked him for trying to grab a bite of fallen bread. That was not the first time the man had kicked him, but the dog decided it would be the last.

From then on, the dog had roamed the countryside, being sure to stay out of the way of Roman soldiers and merchant carts. Now and then a woman would feed him scraps, and sometimes he would dash into a yard and steal a hen. But that was before his knee had gone so bad he had to limp on three legs. Even more important than food was water. The dog knew he had to find some soon, or he would be too weak to go on.

In the distance he heard a splash and his head jerked up. If memory served him, the river was not far from the road, before the path to Cana turned toward the hills. The dog limped off in the direction of the splash. He could almost taste the cool water, and his tongue curled as if he were already lapping at the river.

A crowd of people stood beside the Jordan River, murmuring like reeds in the wind. The dog picked his way between dirty bare feet, trying not to get kicked again. At last he made it to the edge of the river and plunged his tongue into the water, cupping it again and again, scooping the water into his dry mouth. It took him a while to slake his thirst, but when he was satisfied, he took a look around.

The dog saw a skinny fellow standing in the river. The water was up to his waist, and his hands were on the shoulders of a tall, brown-bearded man. The skinny one said something softly to the other man, then shoved him down under the river surface so that nothing but the tall man's long dark hair could be seen floating on the water. The dog yelped in alarm. Surely the people in the crowd would rescue the man from drowning. He would have done it himself, if not for his bad leg.

People were pointing and calling out as the tall man stood up again, his wet robe clinging to his muscular body. The dog saw a bright ray of sunlight break through the clouds in the east and come to rest on the shining wet head of the tall man, who some of the people whispered was named Yeshua. The skinny man said something about the Spirit of God blessing his beloved son, but the words made no sense to the dog. He was just glad the man named Yeshua had not drowned.

He liked the way the man smiled and held up one hand, scattering drops of water. The dog felt a pleasant, tingling warmth in his bad leg as Yeshua's hand reached toward the crowd. When Yeshua came out of the river, the dog limped over to him. Following an urge he could not understand, the dog lay down at the man's feet and licked them.

"And who are you, little fellow?" said Yeshua, stooping to stroke the dog's back. "I see your leg hurts. Let's fix that." His hand moved down to caress the dog's leg, then rested on the kneecap, moving it back into place.

"I will call you Cherem, the selfless one. You are devoted beyond the devotion of men."

Cherem looked into the man's face and felt the pain go away. He stretched out his leg, shook it, and then jumped up, putting his forepaws on Yeshua's shoulders, as he had seen the man in the river do. He wanted to lick the bearded face in gratitude, but thought that might be too bold. Instead, he put his head down and again licked Yeshua's foot. A flash of joy jumped through him, as if he had just been given a fine bone with lots of meat on it. When the man stood up, his wet robe brushed against the dog's nose. Cherem wagged his tail so hard it felt as if it would fly off. He gave a little leap, as he used to do when he was a puppy. Yeshua looked down at him and laughed.

"This dog needs food," he said, and one of the women on the riverbank stepped forward with a piece of cooked chicken. "Thank you," he said, bending to put the chicken in Cherem's open mouth. "And the dog thanks you too."

As Yeshua started to move away up the path to the road, Cherem stood looking after him. His tail wagged more slowly, and his head hung toward the ground. He wanted to follow the group of men and women who surrounded Yeshua. But they had closed around the man they called the Master, and Cherem couldn't see him anymore. Even if he couldn't see the Master, the dog could taste his scent on the air and ground. He meant to follow that scent wherever it led him.

He pursued Yeshua until the group around the Master grew small, and the path up to Cana grew steeper. Now only one woman and a few men followed the Master, and one of them picked up a stone to drive

Cherem away. In spite of the stone-thrower Cherem trotted closer. Suddenly Yeshua looked around and saw him.

"So you're still with me?"

His friends made shooing motions, and tried to drive the animal away.

"Let him come," Yeshua said, holding out his hand to the dog. "Men could learn a lot from him about gratitude."

"But Master, a dog is unclean," said a big man the others called Peter. "So the priests tell us."

"And they say the same thing about women after childbirth," observed the woman who had fed Cherem and now stood near the Master. "Talk about gratitude."

Her name was Mary, and Cherem liked the way she smelled, as if she were a field full of flowers and fresh grass. He also liked the way she slipped him bits of food when the others weren't looking.

Yeshua laughed. "We aren't made unclean by what happens to us or by who we are," he said. "Only by what comes out of our hearts and mouths. This dog,

Cherem, will be one of us from now on. May all my disciples be as pure of heart as he is. And I tell you, my friends, that the pure of heart are the ones who will see God."

As far as Cherem was concerned, he was seeing all of God he needed to see as he looked at Yeshua. He sniffed the breeze and shivered with delight as his Master's scent entered his nose. It was the sweetest he had ever tasted, and he felt he could live on it like air.

Wedding Feast

Chapter Two
Healings

Yeshua let his new dog stay close beside him as he and his followers walked the dusty path to Cana. As the group looked at the town from a distance, one of them remarked on how small the town seemed. Another said it was like all other small towns, not a place anyone would remember. The houses had the usual flat roofs and whitewashed walls. Cherem wondered if dogs were allowed inside. He hoped that he hoped he could sit under a table, where he might find some bits of food.

The group of Yeshua's friends was greeted by a man standing at the door of a small house. The Master's feet were washed by a servant, and he went into the cool, dark interior of the home. So many people were gathered there, eating and drinking, that Cherem was able to sneak in and find a place under the heavily laden table without being noticed and shooed out.

Having consumed all the crumbs of bread and morsels of lamb he could find, Cherem looked out from under the table and saw Yeshua bless a newly married couple.

A tall, gray-haired woman with a blue cloak came to Yeshua and put her hand on his shoulder, drawing him away from the others. Cherem trotted over to his Master and stood next to him as he talked to the woman.

"They've run out of wine," she said. "You know, son, that they're poor, and couldn't afford to serve wine to the wedding guests, let alone the friends you brought with you. The host had to pour a lot of water in what wine he had. It was a great embarrassment to him."

"Mother, it is not yet my time to work miracles," Yeshua said. "Do you want to send me on this path too soon? You know how it will end."

The blue-cloaked woman looked for a long time into his eyes, and then turned toward the host. "Do whatever he tells you," she said.

Yeshua told the host to pour water into tall jars, and then held out his hands, murmuring a blessing.

Cherem did not know what wine was, but thought that anything the Master blessed would have to taste good. He looked up at Yeshua and wagged his tail very hard, knowing something important had happened. All the people were whispering to each other and pointing at Yeshua.

The host tasted what was in the jars and smiled. "It's much better wine than I served before. People will say I held off the best wine until the end."

And people did say so. Still, they were happy with what Yeshua had done, and drank every bit of the wine. Yeshua joined in the dancing, but took just a small taste of the wine and that only because his host insisted. Cherem sat by the wall, his tail thumping the clay floor. He watched his Master dance, glad to see him happy. For Cherem, to hear Yeshua laugh was better than any gift he could imagine. He could taste his Master's joy and be as satisfied as if he had been filled with food.

A few days later, Yeshua and his followers went to another house, where they were well-fed, and Yeshua talked to the people who crowded the room. Despite the lateness of the hour, no one wanted to leave, since Yeshua had started healing the sick. Blind men could suddenly see. Deaf women could hear. Little children dying of fever sat up and laughed under the blessing of his hands.

Cherem heard a noise above him and jumped to his feet, barking in alarm. Through a hole in the roof, he saw some men lowering another man on a bed. The man was as thin and bony as Cherem, and his legs looked even weaker than his body. One leg was crooked, just as Cherem's had been. The Master quieted his dog with a gesture and stood beside the bent man.

"Your sins are forgiven," Yeshua said, holding his hand out to the man. "Be happy."

A few people in the room murmured at his words, wondering how Yeshua could forgive sins as only God could do. But the Master looked at them with one eyebrow raised.

"You think it's easier to forgive sins than to say 'get up and walk'? Watch and see."

Yeshua laid a hand on the man's crooked leg and stroked it gently, a touch that Cherem knew well. The man moved his leg cautiously, and then beamed up at the Master.

"You can walk now," Yeshua said, smiling. "Carry your bed with you. Go to your own house, and give thanks to God."

The people who had murmured against Yeshua were abashed and said nothing more. Cherem looked hard at them and remembered their look and their smell. If they came near Yeshua again, he told himself, he would growl at them and scare them away.

"Peace, Cherem," said Yeshua, reaching down to touch his dog's head. "Love your enemies and mine. It's one of the lessons my followers must learn."

Let the children come

TAMANS

Chapter Three
Teachings

The next day the Master took his friends farther up the hill, away from the town. He was going to tell them some stories, he said. Yeshua taught lessons in his stories, so his hearers would not have to be learned in order to understand. Cherem enjoyed the stories, since sometimes they had food in them. He heard the story about how Yeshua's friends needed to be like leaven in bread and licked his lips. He was not sure how to be leaven, but he very much liked bread, especially with goat cheese on it.

Some of the people who had been at the wedding followed the little group, and so did a number of curious townsfolk. A few dogs trailed them, hoping for something to eat in case the people stopped for lunch. Cherem trotted beside Yeshua, often glancing back at the other dogs, wanting to growl at them if they came too close.

Then he remembered what his Master had said and sighed. Even these dogs must be given a chance to enjoy the Master's presence, if he had understood Yeshua rightly. When one came close, Cherem nosed him in a friendly way, and allowed the other dog to lie down beside him at Yeshua's feet, when the Master finally seated himself on a stone.

Cherem listened as Yeshua spoke, hearing the word 'blessed,' many times, but not knowing quite what it meant. Since Yeshua said it so often, he thought it must mean something good. He would like to be blessed, and figured it was something like being fed a treat or stroked on his belly by Yeshua's gentle hand.

"Blessed are the kind, blessed are the humble," the Master said. And Cherem determined that he would be kind. Being a dog, he was already humble, but there was more to Yeshua's lesson than that. He would have to be peaceful and not bark so much. Cherem looked at the dog next to him, who was falling asleep, his grizzled nose on his forepaws. Instead of nudging him awake, Cherem decided to let him be. He even put a piece of bread beside the old dog's head, so the poor fellow would have something to eat when he woke up. Yeshua looked down at Cherem and smiled at him, which was all the reward the dog could want. He knew he was blessed without being told so.

While Yeshua was resting on a hillside, some mothers and children approached him. The children were making a lot of noise, laughing and talking. Cherem jumped up, wagging his tail. He hoped the children would chase him, for he loved to be chased. He ran round and round Yeshua, then faced the children, his rump raised and his elbows on the ground, knowing the children would understand he wanted to play. Yeshua's friends were angry and waved their arms in the air.

"Don't bother the Teacher," they cried. "He doesn't want to waste his time on children."

Cherem shook his head, thinking that probably they believed Yeshua didn't want to waste his time on dogs either.

"Let the children come," Yeshua said, looking ready for fun, as he often did when Cherem took a play-posture. "If you could be more like them, you'd be happier. Sit on my lap, child," he said to one little boy. "Gather around me, all of you. Would you like to hear a story?"

And he told them a story about a shepherd boy who went looking for a lost sheep. The boy was supposed to bring all the sheep in his pasture home at night. One was missing, a very small one, and the boy felt sad, thinking how scared the little sheep must be.

Cherem understood, for many were the nights he had hidden in the wilderness, not knowing if he would ever find a friend. Then the boy left all the grown-up sheep, knowing they could find their way home, and he looked for the lamb. When he found the lamb, he put it on his shoulders and carried it back to the safe place where all the sheep slept.

Cherem liked the story as much as the children did, for it made him remember how Yeshua had found him and loved him. When he sent the children back to their mothers, Yeshua told them he loved them just as the boy had loved his little lamb. And as Yeshua loves me, Cherem said to himself, glad that his Master had told the children that they were loved. He hoped they would always remember that, just as he would.

Yeshua led his friends to the sea, where one of them, Peter, had a fishing boat that would take them across to another town. Cherem had never been on a boat, and hung back at first. He felt the wind pick up and looked with anxious eyes at the waves breaking on the rocky shore. But Yeshua urged him forward, calling him a brave dog when Cherem climbed into the boat. Cherem didn't feel brave at all and huddled at the Master's feet. Peter pushed off with a long paddle, and the boat quickly sailed out on the waves, pitching and tossing until Cherem felt a little sick to his stomach.

Yeshua was tired after all his talking and did what Cherem wanted to do. The Master went to sleep, laying his arm on the side of the boat and his head on his arm. The boat rocked more and more. Cherem moaned softly and tucked his head between Yeshua's sandals, closing his eyes so he couldn't see the gray clouds heavy with rain, scudding low in the sky. He wanted to wake the Master up, but felt it was not his place. If dogs hated to be waked up, Cherem figured, humans must hate it even more.

Peter finally yelled out as the sail bellied, and the little boat nearly turned over. "Master, we're going down. Wake up before we all die."

Jumping to his feet, Cherem felt Yeshua stir, and none too soon. Thunder boomed and lightning lit the sky, streaking the gray clouds. Cherem peered over the side of the boat and dropped his tail between his legs in terror at the sight of high, white-capped waves surging around them.

He stayed close to Yeshua, thinking that if the boat went down, he might be able to drag his Master to safety. Cherem's swimming skills were strong. He had crossed the Jordan many times and felt himself to be equal to the sea. To save Yeshua, he would risk anything. He glanced up at his Master and at once realized that nothing needed to be done. Lying down again at the feet of Yeshua, he tucked his back feet under his chin, making a perfect circle of his body. Yeshua was in charge, he thought drowsily. Nothing to fear.

"Peter, have you so little faith?" Yeshua said, his voice as quiet as if he were in a field picking corn. Holding up his hands and lifting his face to the elements, Yeshua murmured, "Hush, now. Be at peace."

Cherem felt a sudden shift in the air and lifted his head to look around him. The waves gentled and the wind stopped blowing his ears back.

"What kind of man is this," Cherem heard one of Yeshua's friends whisper, "that even the wind and the sea obey him?"

Cherem could have told them. The Master was a man like no other. His words were one with his action, bringing peace and calm where before there had been chaos and fear. If Yeshua's friends could understand as he did, Cherem thought, they would have more faith in the Master. He would try to show them what faith was, by being a perfect servant to Yeshua. Maybe they could learn from a dog what they could not learn on their own.

Once they had reached the shore, the men in the boat seemed to forget all about what Yeshua had done. All they could think of was getting away from the water that had almost drowned them. They ran onto the beach, pulling the boat with them. Yeshua stood on the rocky shore, reaching down to pat Cherem's head.

"Ask, and you'll receive," he said, as much to the dog as to his other friends. "Trust me, and I will not fail you."

Cherem let out a single sharp bark, wanting to let the Master know that he trusted and believed. Trust was his strong suit. Of the others, who were standing on the beach in a circle, he could not be sure. They talked and gestured, happy to be safe but not sure how their safety had been accomplished. They glanced back at Yeshua and Cherem, their brows furrowed. They looked as if they were afraid to believe, and perhaps, Cherem thought, they were. As for him, he would believe Yeshua could do anything, and he would trust the Master as long as there was life in him.

Although the dog trusted Yeshua, he knew many others did not. He was therefore very surprised by what happened one day when Yeshua went with a Roman soldier into Capernaum, at the man's request. The soldier was an important person, and many followed him. Cherem knew from experience that soldiers were careless about where they put their feet. He kept out of their way, even while he stayed close to Yeshua.

"My servant is shaking with fever and in pain," the man said to the Master. "I fear he's about to die. Please, sir, come with me and heal him. I know you need only say the word and my servant will be healed. When I tell someone to do something, he does it. So I know what power is. I know that you, sir, have more power than I could dream of."

Yeshua stopped on the path and laid his hand on the man's shoulder, though his followers muttered that the soldier was not a child of Israel. "I have found no faith greater than the faith of this Roman," Yeshua said. "Many will come from other places than Israel to enter into my kingdom. He is the first. Centurion, go home. Your servant will greet you at the door."

Cherem was glad to hear these words, for he wanted as many humans as possible to enter the kingdom Yeshua spoke of so often. That was what his Master wanted, so the dog wanted it too.

But those who did not love others as Yeshua taught would not enter his kingdom. Cherem learned that when the Master and his friends ran into two men possessed by devils. At least, that is what Yeshua's friends said, when they saw the filthy, naked men shrieking at Yeshua. The Master's friends pointed at them, saying the men were possessed by devils. That was why they hid behind crumbling, aged tombs that were houses of death.

"Why do you come to torment us, Yeshua of Nazareth," the men cried, scratching themselves through their long, matted hair. "No one can pass this way unless they serve the devils in us."

Yeshua stopped walking, and Cherem stood in front of him, growling softly, letting the men know to come no nearer.

"I serve only God," Yeshua said, his voice calm. "Should I send away the devils that possess you, so you can serve God, too?"

The fierce, angry men looked at each other as if they didn't know what to reply. Then they cried out in terror. "Yeshua, you who are the Son of God! Why do you come to torment us?"

Holding out his hands to them, Yeshua said, "I release these poor men from their suffering. You evil spirits will leave them alone from now on."

The men's voices were harsh and ugly, not sounding like human voices at all. "Then send us into that herd of swine feeding over near that cliff."

"Go," the Master said. And when the evil spirits left them, the two men knelt down on the ground at his feet, their faces happy as the faces of children.

The swine began squealing and trampling each other, pushing forward until all the animals had fallen over the cliff into the sea. The men who had tended them ran into town, screaming just like their pigs. Cherem wondered who was worse off, the swineherds or the swine. He had never eaten the meat of a pig, since he had spent his life among people who would not eat pigs. He wondered if it was because pigs were smart and had feelings, as dogs did. That, Cherem felt, would be a good reason not to eat them.

Yeshua and his friends decided not to go into that town but to camp where they were, near the tombs. Death was nothing to be afraid of, according to the Master. That night, Cherem was uneasy and paced back and forth from the camp to the road. He could hear the sound of men's voices in the distance. Soon the men came near the Master's camp and called to him.

"Go away from our coast," they begged Yeshua. "You have destroyed our way of life. We can't raise pigs anymore. Who knows what you might destroy next? Please, leave us, and go back to the Jews."

Yeshua nodded, but did not speak. He went back to the boat and gestured to Peter that they should cross the sea again.

"These men will no longer tempt the children of Israel with forbidden meat," he said. "I wanted to bless them, but they fear blessing. They want to run from God, not know him. It's easier to run."

Cherem put his head in Yeshua's lap as the boat set out. His Master looked back at the people who didn't want him and shook his head sadly. It was hard, Cherem knew, to be driven away. He wanted his Master to know that even if men rejected him, there was one who would be faithful, no matter what.

'I will always be your dog,' he said to Yeshua, without using words.

"I know," Yeshua replied, scratching Cherem behind the ears, the dog's favorite place to be touched. "You and I are together for life."

Cherem rescues Peter

Chapter Four
Awakenings

Peter was a fisherman, but on this particular night, he had had no luck. His nets came up empty every time. Finally he brought the boat back to shore and got out. Yeshua put a hand on Peter's arm.

"Go out and try again," he said. "Cherem will go with you."

The friends of Yeshua were exhausted, and some of them slept on the beach. But Peter and a few others climbed back into the boat. They went out some distance before Peter let down his nets, explaining to his brother that Yeshua had told him to keep fishing. As he spoke, Peter rolled his eyes, letting his brother know that he didn't for a moment think he would catch anything.

Cherem was offended at the eye-rolling, since he himself would never have questioned an order of the

Master. All at once the nets were full of wiggling, shining little fish, and Peter could hardly haul his heavy catch into the boat.

Cherem suddenly noticed that Yeshua was no longer waiting for them on the shore. Suddenly he turned his head and spied Yeshua near the boat, standing on the surface of the water. The dog let out a sharp bark to alert the men beside him. Then he tensed his body, ready to jump out of the boat and swim. If Yeshua needed rescuing, Cherem thought, his dog should be on the job.

"Stay in the boat, Cherem," Peter ordered. "Don't touch my fish. Master, wait! I want to go with you."

Peter was so excited that he didn't seem to understand there was water all around him. He climbed out of the boat and started walking on the water, his eyes fixed on Yeshua. All at once he seemed to realize he was on water, not on land.

"Master, help," he cried, his mouth filling with water. "I'm going down."

Yeshua shook his head. "You might have more faith, Peter. First, you didn't think any fish would come into your net. Then you thought you couldn't walk to me on the water. And when you thought that, of course you sank."

Gesturing to his dog, Yeshua called out, "Go, Cherem. Jump in and save Peter."

Cherem knew that whatever Yeshua said was more important than the order Peter had given him. So he leaped into the water and swam to the drowning man. Peter was a lot bigger than the dog, but Cherem had faith that the Master would strengthen him for the task. And Yeshua must have, since Cherem was able to drag Peter to the boat.

Yeshua strolled across the waves as if they were no more than rippling sand. He got into the boat and slapped Peter on the back until the man coughed out the last of the water in his lungs.

"Good job, Cherem," he said to his dog, as Cherem shook the water off himself. "Now Peter, what would you say to becoming another kind of fisherman?"

"I don't know," gasped Peter. "What kind?"

"From now on," Yeshua said, "you will catch people, not fish."

"What if the people don't want me to catch them?" Peter sat up slowly and squeezed the water out of his hair.

"Some will, some won't," Yeshua said. "Your job is just to tell them my good news. Heal them and love them. God will do the rest."

Cherem wondered if Peter were up to the task Yeshua had set him. The fisherman seemed too quick to speak and act, rather like Cherem himself. Yeshua had often told his friends not to judge anyone. He said that people tended to judge others for exactly the faults they themselves had. Cherem hung his head. Here he was, despite the Master's message, thinking bad thoughts about Peter for mistakes he himself had made. Yeshua smiled down at him, and Cherem knew the Master was pleased that at least one follower, his dog, understood his teaching.

Yeshua got in trouble again, as soon as their boat landed back on the soil of Judah. He was invited to dinner with a rich man who had collected more taxes than he should have. Cherem didn't understand all that this man, Zechariah, had done wrong, but gathered that no one liked him. The dog tried to stand between Yeshua and the short, plump tax collector, but Yeshua reached out to the man anyway. Wanting to tell his Master that this man smelled as bad as a long-dead fish, Cherem whimpered and leaned against his Master's knee.

"It's all right, Cherem," Yeshua said. "Zechariah is going to be our host at dinner. He'll have a bone for you."

The dog subsided, remembering his Master's words about not thinking badly of others. He trotted meekly beside Yeshua all the way to the tax collector's house. As they walked up to Zechariah's mansion, many people gathered around and murmured against Yeshua.

"Why does he eat with sinners?" the crowd asked Yeshua's friends. "Doesn't he know that Zechariah has stolen our money?"

Yeshua paused before going into the house and turned to face the crowd. "You need to understand," he said, "I've come to heal sinners. Healthy people don't need a doctor. Still, I want you to look into your own hearts, you who hate this man. God asks you to have mercy, not just make sacrifices. Have mercy on Zechariah, and it will be for you as if I had come to dwell in your house."

After that, the crowd went away, and Cherem followed the Master into the tax collector's home, looking forward to the promised bone. He didn't know how long he slept after gnawing on the bone Zechariah's servant gave him. Yeshua might need his protection, and here he was asleep on the job. Hearing a commotion at the door, Cherem leaped to his feet, bumping his head against the low table. A man who looked like a king had come to the tax collector's home, announced by a number of attendants dressed in rich clothing.

The man didn't act like a king. He fell at Yeshua's feet and began to cry. "Master, my daughter is dead. But come to my house anyway and touch her. That's all you need to do, and she'll live."

Cherem wondered what this important man would do if Yeshua could not bring the girl back from the dead. Would he be angry? True, his Master had brought a person back to life before. Still, if Cherem knew anything about death, he knew it was not a small matter, like fixing a kneecap. But Yeshua got up right away and said goodby to the tax collector, thanking him for his food. Like all the followers of Yeshua, the tax collector tagged along behind the Master and his friends, as they went to the house of the important man.

Throughout the town, news had spread that Jairus, the rich man whose daughter had died, had asked Jesus to come and bring her back from wherever the dead went. People came running after the Master and called out questions. To Cherem, they didn't seem friendly. Head lowered, the dog stood between Yeshua and the crowd.

"The girl's dead," they cried out. "What do you think you can do, Yeshua of Nazareth? Are you God himself? Who else could raise the dead?"

"The girl isn't dead," Yeshua said to the crowd. "She's just sleeping, as do all the dead before God gathers them to himself."

The people laughed at him, calling him names, and Cherem felt the hackles rise on his back as he growled a warning. Let one of these rude people come near his Yeshua, and that man's ankle would be raw meat. So Cherem swore to himself, staying close to his Master as they entered the house, an even grander one than the tax collector's. This man with the dead daughter must be very important indeed, Cherem thought, looking at the tall columns lining the entryway and the fine silk brocade hanging at the windows.

Death was familiar to Cherem, since he had seen other dogs lying lifeless beside the road. Once a dog had gone still, he would not move again. That was a fact. Death was the end. Cherem was a realist and knew that when life was finished, nothing more could be expected.

The important man and his weeping wife ushered Yeshua into the room where their dead daughter lay on a table. Already the mourners had gathered with their musical instruments, which gave off sad, ugly sounds. Women wailed and ripped their clothes. To Cherem, the scene looked hopeless. The little girl, round-cheeked and pretty even in death, would not move again. Cherem nosed her arm, which hung from the table, pale and cold. Yeshua might as well forget about this healing, the dog thought. The child was not coming back. Like the dogs he had seen beside the road, she was dead as a stone.

Yeshua sent everyone but Cherem to the far side of the room. Then he leaned over and breathed on the young girl's body, his face close to hers. The dog pressed against the girl's arm and felt it turn warm and move.

"Sit up, child, and take my hand. Your father's waiting for you," Yeshua said.

The girl did as he told her. She looked sleepy and rubbed her eyes as Yeshua led her to her parents. Cherem trotted behind them, tail wagging and head high. Just let anyone say again that his Master couldn't wake the dead.

As if making the dead live again weren't enough to prove Yeshua was God, the next day he shocked a huge crowd of people by making food appear out of nowhere. Cherem and everyone else knew that food was hard to come by. Most people lived on the edge of starvation, and if you were a dog, you starved more often than not. So, food was important. Like water, bread was life.

With all Yeshua's friends and a multitude of men, women, and children, Cherem climbed a hill where everyone rested and listened to the Master's words, which Cherem never tired of hearing. He sat at his Master's feet and perked his ears forward, not wanting to miss anything.

"Come to me and rest, you who are tired and worried," Yeshua said. "You'll find my burden is light."

Cherem knew what Yeshua meant. Nothing was hard if the Master was right there, loving you. Still, hunger was gnawing at his belly, and words were not food. Cherem looked up at Yeshua, who had finally finished talking to the crowd.

"I know you're hungry," Yeshua said to the hundreds of people gathered around him. "Has anyone brought food along?"

Cherem whimpered a little and hoped somebody would come forward. His stomach felt as if it was smashed against his spine, and it ached. A little boy got up and put two small loaves and five tiny tilapia fish into Yeshua's hands.

"Is this all there is?" Yeshua looked out over the crowd. "Well then, the boy's gift will be our food." The Master closed his eyes and spoke in a low voice, "Father, give us today our daily bread."

All around them, people slipped open their pouches and pulled out what they had brought with them. Cherem could hardly believe his eyes. The pouches seemed to hold endless riches—cold meats, bread, goat cheese. The dog licked his lips. It was a feast. Yeshua held out his hands, blessing the boy's small gift, and it turned into a mountain of food that would grace a rich man's wedding. People rose and added their own food to the pile. Cherem was unsure what Yeshua had brought forth and what had come from the people themselves.

"The kingdom of heaven is like yeast," Yeshua said as he blessed the food. "Give what you have been given and much will come of it. Sow your seed, and it will grow up among the weeds. Many will be fed from your fields."

People ate until they were stuffed, and so did Cherem. When they were done, they went around with baskets, collecting every scrap to take home with them. Some people spoke of the food as manna in their wilderness, but Cherem did not understand what that might be. To him, it was just food. Yeshua could be depended on to provide what his friends needed, and Cherem was glad to be one of them.

About this time, Yeshua heard that a beloved friend of his, Lazarus, was very sick. The sisters of Lazarus wanted Yeshua to come to their home and cure him. Cherem remembered these sisters because during Yeshua's last visit to their home, they had had a fight. Martha had been busy in the kitchen, getting all red and sweaty as she cooked dinner. She tossed him some scraps, so he tended to take her side when Mary refused to help with the cooking and serving. Mary was busy learning from the Master, sitting at his feet just as the disciples did.

Martha finally lost her temper and called from the kitchen door, "Master, my sister should come and help me, not sit around like a man, doing nothing."

Yeshua laughed softly, not wanting to upset Martha further.

"Let Mary be," he said. "She will help you later, and so will I. For now, she has chosen to stay with me, and that's a good thing." Martha was embarrassed and went back to serving the food. When Yeshua ate dinner, he told Martha how fine her food tasted, so she felt better and gave Cherem extra scraps.

Now the fighting between the two women was over, for Mary had learned from Yeshua that the best thing she could do for him was to serve others. Since their brother had been sick, the two women had looked after him and the household together, and Mary no longer shirked her duties.

The women both looked pale and miserable when Yeshua and his friends, including Cherem, arrived at their home.

"Master, if you had been here sooner, our brother Lazarus would not have died," Martha burst out, tears running down her cheeks.

Yeshua stood still, his eyes wet. "So Lazarus is gone? My sisters, I grieve with you. Take me where you have laid him."

They went through a vineyard to a stone tomb which was cut into a cliff. Yeshua made everyone stay back except Cherem. Together they went to the tomb of Lazarus. Cherem wanted to lick the tears from his

Master's eyes, but couldn't reach that far. So he licked his foot instead. The dog felt Yeshua's sadness well up inside him as if it had been his own.

"Push the stone aside," Yeshua called to Peter and James, two big, strong disciples. "I will go closer to the grave."

The people were very afraid of death and seemed to think it might be contagious. They urged Yeshua not to go near the dead body, but the Master was firm.

"Move the stone," he repeated, and the two disciples did it, with loud groans and much effort.

Yeshua motioned them away and stood right in front of the open grave. "Lazarus, come out," he called in a voice so loud, it scared Cherem. Yeshua's words echoed in the rocky hollow where the body was. The dog whimpered and lay down, putting his paws over his nose. The air from the grave smelled sweet and sick, the worst kind of smell.

Out of the stone tomb came a white, shrouded figure that stood in the sunlight, pulling the cloth from around its face. Yeshua ran to the man and hugged him, not caring about the awful smell. Cherem hung back, wanting as little to do with death and bad smells as possible.

Martha and Mary came running too, and all four of them stood together, hugging and laughing. The humans didn't seem to care about the smell, but Cherem kept his distance, not liking it at all. Once the sisters of Lazarus had cleaned their brother up and put fresh clothes on him, the smell went away, and Cherem danced around the once-dead man, celebrating his return to life. Lazarus was generous with food, since he was happy not to be dead any more, and lavished scraps on the dog as he talked to Yeshua about what being dead was like.

The Master listened carefully as his friend talked, and when Lazarus fell silent, Yeshua said, "In my father's house are many happy places that are prepared for you. Don't fear those who can kill the body, but only those who kill the soul. Death is just a moment between this life and the Father's paradise. So don't be sad when I die. Understand, I will die so that you can live. "

The friends of Yeshua looked worriedly at each other, for they had no doubt viewed death as Cherem had. To them, death looked like the end. But Yeshua had told them it was only the beginning of life. Cherem believed him, since the dog had seen butterflies come out of gray, dead husks and fly off into the sky. He had seen several people come back to life and knew that nothing was as it seemed. The larger world was the real one, and the small world that men and animals sensed was only a piece of the big picture.

Chapter Five
Deepenings

"Can we be first in heaven, seated beside you?" asked two of his followers. Their eyes glittered with hope for advancement. Cherem could hardly believe how bold they were. He himself would have bitten off his own paw before insulting his Master this way.

"It's not for me to give you these positions of glory," Yeshua said. "Those who are last now will be first in the kingdom of God. Try to be last, to be humble. The kingdom I rule is the opposite of the kingdom you know here on earth."

Cherem wagged his tail, glad to hear that the humble would have a place in the kingdom Yeshua spoke of so often. He understood that Yeshua was turning the world upside down.

Some people didn't want their world any different. They liked it just the way it was. And they had no wish to change themselves, either. They did what their laws said to do, and if there was more that God might want for them, they didn't care to hear about it. Yeshua was telling them to change, and they wanted to stay as they were. It was easier.

Cherem understood how they felt. It had been easier at the beginning of his life, when his mother fed him from her body. When he grew up, he had to learn how to seek his own food. That was how he had found Yeshua, by growing up.

About the time when Yeshua told his followers he would have to die in order for them to live, he took them to a high mountain called Tabor. It looked like a camel's hump. Cherem was not happy at the thought of climbing such a high, rocky place, but if Yeshua wanted him to, he would do it.

Only a few of Yeshua's friends went with them, and Cherem got the feeling that what they were going to do on the mountain was too much for most of the

Master's followers to grasp. The weather was hot and when they got to the top of Mt. Tabor, everyone except Yeshua lay down on the ground, panting and sweating. Yeshua went off to pray, since he didn't seem to be tired, and Cherem went with him.

Suddenly a bright ray of sunlight plunged through a cloud and lit up the figure of the Master. Cherem jumped to his feet and barked. He wanted to be sure Yeshua knew something strange was going on. Drawn by the dog's barks, the Master's friends came running, then fell down on their faces, full of fear. Like Cherem, they could see glowing forms of two men on either side of Yeshua.

"Moses," Peter called out. "It must be Elijah and Moses! Let's make shrines to these holy ones."

Cherem whined and put his long nose between his front paws. Whoever these fiery friends of Yeshua were, they were frightening. He didn't want to make shrines. He just wanted them to go away so he could have his Master back again. After a while, they did go away, and only Yeshua remained.

"Don't be afraid," he said to his friends. "And don't tell anyone what you've seen until I have risen from the dead."

There it was again, Cherem thought, trembling with fear worse than he had felt when the two bright strangers had appeared beside the Master. Yeshua was saying he would die. No, Cherem thought, let me die, but not him.

The Master began to travel south, toward the great city where the Temple was. Cherem had no idea what a temple might be or why anyone would want to go there. For him, being with Yeshua on the open road was enough. But Yeshua told his friends that this journey was one he must make.

He said something very strange to them. "Unless you take me into yourselves like food, you will not have my life in you."

Cherem whimpered at hearing these words, since the very thought of biting his Master made him want to run away and hide.

One of Yeshua's friends said he couldn't stand the thought of eating the flesh of his Master. Some others took a long, sad look at Yeshua and departed.

"Try to understand," Yeshua said. "I am the very source of what you are. When you eat my flesh and drink my blood, I give you my life."

Cherem understood a little, but dimly. When Yeshua gave him his dinner, that food became part of the dog's body. The grain of the bread, the meat of animals—all these were a gift, standing for the gift of the whole creation, all the life on earth. Yeshua was the whole world, offered up on God's table. Who could say no to consuming such a gift, such a feast? Why would anyone want to? Cherem wanted to be part of his Master, however that could be done. Only Yeshua could make it happen. Only Yeshua could give up his own body for the life of the world, so the world could learn how to love as he did.

Many of Yeshua's followers murmured to each other and backed off, acting as if they had somewhere else they needed to be. Cherem wanted to tell them, just take his word for it. Have faith and open your mouths like little birds to take what he gives you. But Cherem had no words.

The Master looked sadly at the followers who stayed. "Will you go away too?"

Cherem wanted to howl. How could anyone want to leave such a one as Yeshua was? He was afraid he might be the only friend the Master had left.

Peter stopped walking and looked into Yeshua's eyes. "Who would we go to?" he asked in a low voice. "You are the one who tells us the truth. For us, there is no one but you."

The friends of Yeshua began to learn what was about to happen, but they couldn't believe it. Cherem understood why. Losing the Master was the worst thing that could happen, and that was what Yeshua was preparing them for. He told them in bits and pieces, knowing they couldn't bear to hear it all at once.

"When the temple falls," he said, "I will rebuild it in three days."

He said these words as they approached the great city of David, the place Yeshua's friends called the holiest on earth.

"Do you mean that the Temple of David, the Great King, will collapse?" Judas demanded. Judas was very concerned about the Temple and the future of the Holy Land that had been King David's.

Cherem could see images of war and death in the mind of Judas. The man wanted Yeshua to lead the people of Israel into a battle against the Roman soldiers. Having seen the fury of soldiers as they killed helpless people, Cherem thought Yeshua would find another way. Murder was not what Yeshua recommended.

"Go ahead of me into Jerusalem," the Master said. "Find me a donkey and tell the owner I need it. The time has come for me to finish my Father's work."

These words confused Cherem, since he thought Yeshua had a lot more to do than he had done so far. Too many people were sick, too many poor, too many dying. Surely, he thought, the Master wasn't done with his work. Judas might have been thinking the same thing. Everyone, including Cherem, was hoping that Yeshua would take charge of the world and turn it into a better place. They wanted life to be easy, wanted Yeshua to make it so. Cherem knew, from seeing the images in Yeshua's mind, that an easy life was not what he had come to give. But even if there were pain, underneath it all, there would be peace. Yeshua had said many times that he had come to give peace, not the peace that the world's goods give, but peace deep in the heart.

Cherem knew that peace from experience. It was the quiet joy of knowing that he was part of Yeshua, that Yeshua was part of him. When he and Yeshua were together, he wanted nothing more. His Master was all there was, all he needed. Cherem wondered if the other followers of Yeshua felt the same way he did, or if they wanted to be important, wanted to be masters themselves, wanted to have everything go their way.

If that was what they wanted, the dog thought, they were likely to be disappointed. Yeshua's idea was that they wouldn't get what they liked, but should like what they got. The moment provided by the Master ought to be enough. For Cherem, it was.

Someone brought a donkey to Yeshua, who sat on it, stroking the animal's neck and speaking to it gently. Cherem knew how the donkey felt. Yeshua was no burden. But in his heart, the dog felt uneasy. As he followed the donkey into the city, Cherem kept his head low, making a moaning sound in his throat. All these people waving palm fronds, screaming a welcome, had no idea who Yeshua was. They thought he would give them power and all kinds of good things. They thought he would act like a king, favoring his friends.

They thought he was a warrior, like King David, someone who would make life pleasant for them. They had no idea he was the food of life, the God-force who drove the sun, the planets, the stars. The one whose touch brought peace to anyone who needed peace. Cherem trotted forward, his heart heavy, his love growing by the minute, his desire to protect his Master driving him into a panic. This place was bad, he thought. This place would be his Master's end. Cherem wanted to bark a warning, but knew he had to stay silent. That was how Yeshua often handled trouble—with silence. But not on this day.

Cherem had never seen Yeshua angry before. When the Master walked into the arcade around the temple, full of tables piled with money, his hands were busy braiding a handful of rope into a whip. In the past, Cherem had been beaten with such a whip, but he wasn't afraid. He knew Yeshua would never hurt him. But who was he going to hit with that whip? The dog stayed at Yeshua's side and kept his tail between his legs.

The Master walked up to a table bigger than the others. Underneath it birds and animals were being kept in cages, packed together so closely they could hardly move. Cherem put his nose against one cage and whined, wanting Yeshua to open the cage and let the poor animals go free.

Yeshua tipped the table over, so coins flew in every direction. Birds in the cages flapped their wings and lambs bleated in fear. Yeshua snapped his whip and kicked open a cage, letting the animals out.

"You really think God wants you to kill helpless creatures because you yourselves are sinners?" he cried out. "God wants mercy, not sacrifice. You've turned my Father's house into a den of thieves. Money and innocent animals cannot buy God's favor. Instead, give to the poor. Open your hearts to the love of God. Wake up."

He went down the row of tables turning over one after another. The priests who were trading animals for money ran away, scared out of their wits. Cherem was scared, too. He had not known that people killed animals because they thought God would bless them for it. For all he knew, next they would start killing dogs. He stayed close to Yeshua, hoping no one would put him in a cage and sell him to be killed.

One lamb went running down the arcade, kicking its rear feet in the air, and a little boy grabbed it. The lamb nuzzled the boy's face, and the boy ran out of the temple, still holding the lamb. Cherem hoped the lamb was now safe. It seemed to him strange that anyone could think killing a lamb would make God happy.

"I will be the lamb of God," Yeshua said to his friends, when he had cleared the moneychangers out of the temple. "I will die for my people. They need to stop killing animals that have done no harm."

The friends of Yeshua looked unhappy. "Master," they said, "you are your people's hope. Lead us against the Romans. Make us strong, the way King David did."

Yeshua shook his head. "I wish you could hear what I'm saying. Unless I die, you can't live. It's that simple. Love is what I've come to teach. Love means you would die for your friends. That's my message. Unless I die, you won't know how much I love you."

Cherem suddenly grasped what Yeshua wanted his friends to know. He gave a little bark of approval and chased his tail in a circle, feeling good. Ever since he had met Yeshua, he had understood what love was. Maybe now the men around Yeshua would understand. His heart felt ready to burst with love for his Master. Sometimes it seemed to him as if he existed only to take joy in being with Yeshua.

His Master had told a woman at her village well that he was living water, better than the kind in the well. That was when Cherem learned that whenever he drank water, he took Yeshua's love into himself. Yeshua was the food he ate, the air he breathed. Yes, Cherem knew what it was to love. And the love he felt for Yeshua would last beyond death itself.

The time of Passover had come, when all the people celebrated being saved by God. Cherem understood what it was to be saved from death and grief because Yeshua had done that for him. The people around him might need a reminder, but the dog didn't. Still, the food at Passover was the best. To be saved and have fine food into the bargain seemed to Cherem a good prospect. He followed Yeshua, close at his Master's heels.

The Master took his friends up a narrow stone staircase that led them into a room with a table and some benches in it. Cherem followed closely behind the others and lay under the table at Yeshua's feet. He was glad everyone was going to eat now. Nothing could please him more. Maybe Yeshua was going to make meat and cheese suddenly appear, as he had before. Cherem wriggled in anticipation, wagging his long, thin tail.

He was surprised when Yeshua took a big bowl of water and a towel and began to wash the feet of his followers. They were surprised too. Usually only a servant washed anyone's feet. But this time Yeshua wanted to teach an important lesson: everyone should be willing to serve everyone else. Yeshua didn't wash Cherem's feet, since he knew his dog already understood the lesson of service. Cherem was just as glad, since he hated to get his feet wet, especially on a cold night like this one.

After the Passover feast, the Master prayed over a loaf of bread and a cup of wine. He asked his Father in heaven to bless this food and drink. Then he said to his friends, "This bread is my body. Eat it and be part of me. Someday you will eat it in my memory."

Cherem shuddered and tucked his head under one paw. Yeshua was telling his friends to do a thing no one could do. He felt a thought coming from the

Master—take me into yourself so that we are One. Eat and drink me like food and wine. Do this always. Never forget that you are mine, and I am yours.

The dog relaxed, now that he understood. Yeshua, as usual, was telling a story with a meaning behind it. He wanted to tell his people that he would be with them, no matter what, that he would feed their hearts and souls with God, with himself. Cherem liked the sound of that. He wanted Yeshua to be part of him forever and was glad Yeshua understood what he wanted. The friends of Yeshua seemed not to understand. One of them got up and went to the door. He and Yeshua looked at each other, their gazes locking.

"Go, and do what you have to do," Yeshua said.

Cherem didn't know what that was, but his heart hurt. Somehow, he felt, that friend was not a friend. For once, the dog didn't feel hungry, but just lay on the floor, his chin resting on Yeshua's foot.

After the meal in the upstairs room, Yeshua led his friends out into the night. Few people were in the streets because they were having their once-a-year

Passover meal, celebrating the time when their ancestors had left the slavery of Egypt. It was Cherem's favorite holy day, since more food was available than anyone could eat. A lot was left over for poor folks and dogs.

Everyone knew the story behind the feast, but only Yeshua knew what was about to happen on this Passover. God had saved the people of Israel from being slaves in those long ago times; Yeshua was going to save them now and forever. He was going to teach them what love really was. It would not be easy.

Cherem hoped he could help to save Yeshua from whatever bad thing was coming. He wished the meal would never end, so his Master would stay safe in the little room. But the time came when they had to leave and go out into the night. The wind had grown cold, and Cherem shivered.

The garden of Gethsemane

Chapter Six

Endings

The garden Yeshua led his friends to was dark, except for a bit of moonlight that shone between gathering clouds. The curved limbs of olive trees drooped, and their pale leaves twisted in the evening breeze. Cherem could feel danger making the hair on his back stand straight up. He stayed close to his Master while the others slept. They had drunk wine at their feast and eaten more than usual. Now they couldn't stay awake.

Cherem was thankful he had not overeaten and was alert. The Master seemed glad of his dog's company and reached down to caress his head. Together, they found a stone slab, large as a table, and Yeshua knelt down beside it, his face in his hands. Cherem sighed, feeling a dark sadness come over him, and pressed close to his Master's side. Maybe, he thought, I'm feeling what my Master feels. That happens a lot. I wish I could feel it for him, so he wouldn't be so sad.

Yeshua's voice was deep and soft. "I don't really want to do this," he said. "But since you ask it of me, Father, I will."

Cherem wasn't sure what Yeshua had to do. But he knew what it felt like to do something you didn't want to do just because someone you loved asked you a favor. Dogs were born knowing how to do that. Whatever Yeshua asked of him, he would do, even if it meant going without food or sleeping on rocks. Even if it meant dying. Cherem hoped that wasn't what Yeshua had to do, but if it was, the Master would not be alone. He could hear voices down below and smell the bodies of men who were sneaking up on Yeshua and his friends. No one but the Master and Cherem seemed to know what was going on.

Suddenly a lot of men came into the garden, and the followers of Yeshua woke up, rubbing their eyes and talking in low voices. Yeshua had asked them to stay awake, but they hadn't. Now they hardly knew what to do. The man Yeshua had sent to do an errand for him grabbed the Master by his cloak and kissed him. Cherem growled and bared his teeth. This kiss did not seem like the good kind.

Peter rushed at the men who surrounded Yeshua, shouting and waving a sword he had snatched from one of the intruders. Although Peter was barely awake, he was trying to do the right thing. He wanted to save his Master, but was not remembering the Master's message. Cherem wished he could explain to Peter that the sword wasn't needed, just as it wouldn't be right for Cherem to bite the soldiers who were surrounding Yeshua.

Instead, they should wait until the Master made clear what he wanted them to do. Peter didn't wait. He charged forward and sliced one soldier's ear off. Cherem picked it up in his mouth, not knowing what to do with it. Certainly eating a human ear was not acceptable behavior for the Master's dog. Yeshua held out his hand, and the dog put the ear into it, glad to be rid of his bloody mouthful.

To everyone's surprise, Yeshua put the man's ear back where it belonged, telling Peter, "Those who live by the sword will die by the sword."

Cherem thought that the Master was probably saying these words to the man who had betrayed him as much as he was saying them to Peter. How many times the dog had heard the betrayer beg Yeshua to fight the Roman soldiers with an army of angels. But that was not the way of the Master. Causing death or hurt to someone else was the world's way. Cherem had seen and felt cruelty enough times to know that. But Yeshua's way was to give up his life for his friends. Again, Cherem sensed, the Master was turning the world upside down.

It was after midnight when the soldiers led Yeshua up the hill to the palace of the chief priests. They were as rich in worldly goods as the Master was poor. Still, Cherem would rather be at Yeshua's side than feasting in the priests' palaces. The followers of Jesus had run away in fear, all except for Cherem, who stayed close by his Master's heels. No one seemed to care if the dog entered the palace. They probably didn't even notice him, since he and Yeshua were surrounded by the temple police.

Cherem was surprised at how many people were milling around the great palace hall, since the streets had been deserted that night. These people, he figured, must be friends of the temple priests. Certainly they were no friends of Yeshua's. They shoved the Master and called out insults. Cherem growled, but Yeshua signaled him to silence. The dog's tail drooped. He wanted to bite every ankle in sight, but knew the Master would not approve. Instead, the dog pressed close against Yeshua's leg and panted, his heart beating so hard that he thought it would jump out of his chest.

Men came forward and said bad things about Yeshua. He had threatened to tear down the temple. He had said he was God. Everyone agreed that Yeshua was guilty of being different from other rabbis and said that he should die. Cherem growled low in his throat, and once again Yeshua held up his hand for silence. He himself would say nothing more. Wanting to behave as his Master did, Cherem became quiet and lowered his head as he followed Yeshua out the door. Now they were surrounded not only by armed guards, but by shouting, threatening crowds of men, the very men who had accused Yeshua of crimes. What crimes, Cherem wondered, since all the Master had done was to heal the sick and teach people how to be kind instead of cruel.

All of them surged down the hill, carrying Yeshua and Cherem with them like flotsam in a flood. As they went, the soldiers beat and cursed Yeshua. It was all Cherem could do to watch, knowing his Master wanted him to do nothing. Yeshua was bleeding from a hundred blows, but staggered on. Cherem whimpered a little, and someone beat him too. He didn't mind, since any blow aimed at him would be one less aimed at Yeshua. He heard the words of the crowd, that Yeshua was going to the Roman ruler, Pilate, who would certainly have him killed.

None of the happy people who had welcomed the Master in Jerusalem a few days before were there now. Only his enemies, who did their dark deeds at night, when good people were sleeping. Cherem wished that he and Yeshua could be back in the garden again, nestled together under a tree. He wanted to keep his Master safe and warm, as he always had. But Yeshua wanted to go forward on this road, and Cherem would try to want that too.

The soldiers jammed a circle of thorns down on Yeshua's head, and Cherem closed his eyes, not wanting to see the blood flow over his Master's face. They were yelling something about crowning Yeshua a king and laughing at him. Cherem remembered that a mean human had poured boiling water on him, when he was only a pup. The man had laughed when Cherem yelped in pain. The dog knew too well what cruelty was, but why someone would want to hurt Yeshua, he did not know. It must be a human thing, he thought, and gave up trying to figure it out.

Cherem tried to get close to his Master, wanting to give him comfort, but there were too many feet in the way. So the dog just sat and waited, making no sound. Finally the soldiers got bored with tormenting Yeshua, since the Master said nothing and didn't cry out, no matter how hard they beat him.

They took Yeshua to Pilate, the Roman governor. Cherem had heard the priests tell the soldiers to be sure Pilate gave Yeshua a death sentence. They said he was a troublemaker for the Jews and would be a troublemaker for Rome if he weren't killed. So Yeshua was brought before the ruler of the land. The priests probably hoped the ruler had no more interest in justice than they did. Yeshua had no one to protect him but his dog, and his dog had been forbidden to help him. His heart pounding with fear, Cherem followed as closely behind his Master as he could.

It was early in the morning, and Pilate had probably been up late having a party. At least he looked to Cherem like most humans looked when they had eaten and drunk too much. Maybe he would let Yeshua go, the dog hoped. That way, the man could go back to bed, which was clearly where he wanted to be. That was where Cherem wanted to be too, with his Master sleeping beside him.

This whole night seemed to him like a bad dream, the kind when you run away from somebody who wants to hurt you. You run and you run, but you can't escape. Yeshua sometimes had to wake Cherem when the dog kicked and moaned in his sleep. Cherem knew this particular bad dream was one he and Yeshua would not wake up from.

"So, who are you?" The Roman governor asked, yawning. A servant brought him a cup, and he drank a lot of whatever was in it.

Yeshua didn't say anything, and the Roman tried again.

"They say you are a king. Well, are you?"

"Yes, but my kingdom, unlike yours, is not of this world." Yeshua replied. "You have nothing to fear from me, and that's the truth."

Pilate laughed and took another swig from his cup. "What is truth?"

Yeshua didn't answer, but just stood there, looking the Roman straight in the eyes, until the other man looked away.

"I don't see what the problem is," Pilate said to the crowd of men behind Yeshua. "He seems to me like a good man. What do you want me to do with him?"

"Crucify him!" the men shouted, shaking their fists."Crucify him!"

Cherem didn't know the word, but caught a picture from their minds. It made him put his tail between his legs and moan. What they wanted to do was worse than any animal would do to another. He had seen this kind of cruelty often, for thousands of Jews had been put to death on crosses along the roads that Cherem travelled with Yeshua. You could hear the victims scream from far away, and they sometimes screamed for days.

This terrible death was what the men had in mind for Cherem's Master, who had healed and loved them. Cherem couldn't believe it. He pushed forward, between the soldiers' sandals and licked his Master's leg. Yeshua looked down at him with a deep, sad line between his eyebrows. He was too sad to smile at his dog, something that had never happened before.

Pilate gestured to a servant, who brought out a dirty, heavyset man and made him stand next to Yeshua.

"You can choose the one you want to crucify," he called out to the crowd. "Barabbas the murderer, or Yeshua."

Cherem thought the Roman had a plan. People would surely rather kill a murderer than a holy man. Pilate must be favoring Yeshua. That was why he was giving the crowd a choice. The dog waited nervously, his eyes on his Master. Maybe this awful night would end well, after all.

"Barabbas," the men yelled, clapping their hands. "We want Barabbas."

Yeshua glanced at the killer with a tired smile. Barabbas looked back at him, and Cherem could tell he was both glad to be free and sorry that Yeshua had to suffer in his place. Barabbas reached out to Yeshua, but some men in the crowd pulled him away. The freed murderer disappeared among them.

If Cherem had been in his place, he would have stayed and insisted that Yeshua be freed instead. But humans tended to think of themselves first and not about saving someone else. Cherem could not understand, since he would gladly have died in Yeshua's place. That was why, he supposed, Yeshua had come to save humans, not dogs. Dogs already knew his message and lived by it.

Cherem looked around him to see if any of the Master's followers were nearby. Maybe they would offer to take Yeshua's place. But none of them were there. Cherem wondered if they had been arrested too, but no, probably they had run away. Yeshua had always told them not to be afraid, but like all humans, when their lives were at stake, that's all they worried about.

The Roman governor looked as if he wanted to forget what had just happened. He dipped his hands into a silver bowl of water and said, "I am not guilty of this good man's death."

Oh, yes you are, Cherem thought, growling and hanging his head low. But so is everybody else. Someday you'll know that. Someday you'll be sorry, just as I am now.

He followed the soldiers who took Yeshua through the crowd. Morning had broken, and some of the good people who loved Yeshua were now in the streets, confused and scared. They followed the soldiers and the prisoner through the city and outside the walls to a hill shaped like a skull. Golgotha, people called it. Cherem had seen it before. As Yeshua and his friends had approached the city a few days ago, the Master had paused at the bare, ugly hill and stared at it. No one asked why they were stopping there, but Cherem had shivered at the sight, knowing this was a bad place, one he wished his Master would stay away from.

The soldiers stripped off Yeshua's clothes and laid him on the wooden cross. What they did next Cherem could not watch. He felt that he himself was dying now and that the pain of his Master was his own. He glanced behind him and saw the mother of Yeshua, standing as close to her son as she was allowed to. The other Marys, one of Magdala, one the sister of Lazarus, stood on either side of her, supporting her because she was too weak with grief to stand up alone. Since he could do nothing for Yeshua, Cherem went to the feet of his Master's mother.

"Look," said one of the Marys. "It's Yeshua's dog. Like us, he wants to be with the Lord until the end. It's the way of dogs."

"And of disciples," said a deeper voice. It was the youngest friend of Yeshua, called John. He stood behind the mother of Yeshua and put his hand on her shoulder. "Let's go closer to him. Now that the cross stands upright, surely the soldiers won't care. They've done what they were told to do."

Cherem followed the little group of Jews to the foot of the cross. He could hardly bear to see his Master's pale face, but this moment might be the last he would ever share with his best friend.

Yeshua looked down at his mother, and she looked up at him. Cherem knew that look; it was the look that said, "I love you" and "Don't be afraid." It was the look that gave Cherem peace, no matter how bad he felt.

Yeshua said a few words, so low Cherem could hardly hear. "Mother, this is your son." He nodded to John, and said, "Son, this is your mother."

Then he looked down at Cherem, and the dog felt his Master's love, like a burst of sunlight at dawn. You don't have to say anything to me, the dog thought. I know you love me.

Cherem closed his eyes. Nothing was left between him and his Master that needed saying.

Just then, dark clouds clashed together and lightning flashed between them. Cherem barely steadied himself as thunder shook the hilltop. At least, he thought it was thunder.

"Earthquake!" people cried, and went running down the hill. "God must be angry with us!"

One of the Roman soldiers stood by Yeshua's cross, hanging onto it so as not to fall. "Surely this man is the Son of God," he cried.

Now you understand, Cherem wanted to reply, if he had had the words. But it's too late.

The soldier who had cried out held up something for Yeshua to drink. Maybe, Cherem thought, the man understood that the Master was thirsty. Yeshua had tried to let them know, but his words were so soft, even Cherem could barely hear.

Instead of drinking, Yeshua looked up at the sky, then down at his friends. "It is finished," he said, his voice strong again. "Into your hands, Father, I give my spirit."

And that's what he did. Cherem watched his Master's head drop to his chest, his body relax, his eyes close. It was, indeed, finished. Cherem threw back his head and howled. His Master was gone.

Hallelujah!

Chapter Seven
Beginnings

The soldiers took the body of Yeshua down from the cross. They had a moment of compassion, letting the Master's mother sit on a rock with Yeshua's body across her knees. Cherem had seen mothers with their children hold them in just the way Mary the Mother held Yeshua, her face against his.

A friend of Yeshua's whom Cherem had not seen for a while came to take the body away. His name was Joseph, and he was rich enough to have a tomb nearby, a tomb big enough to be a whole house for an ordinary person. John carried Yeshua's body into Joseph's tomb and covered it with a long white cloth. Nobody noticed the dog that crept into the cave and hid behind a rock.

Cherem lay quietly, hearing a big stone being rolled in front of the tomb. He was sure he would die in this place, since there was no air, no water, and no food. That was fine with him. To die beside the body of Yeshua was all he could hope for.

A day and night went by, though the dog could not measure them, and he lay as close as he could get to the stone slab on which Yeshua rested. Suddenly, just as Cherem's eyes drifted closed in what he supposed was his final sleep, a bright flash of light filled the tomb, and the dog's eyes flew open. Something big was happening, Cherem thought. Something that had never happened before. It was a moment greater than the time Moses and Elijah stood beside Yeshua on Mount Tabor. Cherem felt his heart leap with joy. His Master sat up on the slab of rock and took the white cloth from his face.

Cherem scrambled to his feet, feeling weak and hungry. He made a small noise, not quite a whimper, but enough to draw Yeshua's attention.

"So, you are here, my friend," Yeshua said, reaching down to pat the dog's head. "You're the only one who's here."

Cherem began to run around the tomb, leaping into the air, tossing his head, yipping like a puppy. He had once thought death was the end, but suddenly it wasn't. Cherem jumped into his Master's arms, taking a leap greater than seemed possible for an old dog. He wanted to tell Yeshua, let's get out of this place and go away together, just you and me.

"I know how you feel," Yeshua said. "But where I'm going you can't go. Not right away. Soon we'll be together always."

The stone that blocked the doorway had been rolled away, and Cherem followed his Master outside. Yeshua stretched, breathed deeply, and smiled down at his dog.

"Hallelujah," he said. "I'm glad that's over, aren't you?"

Cherem nodded his agreement. Both of them saw a woman walking up the hill to the tomb. It was Mary of Magdala. She carried flowers in her arms.

"Are you the gardener?" she said to Yeshua.

"Mary," Yeshua said, and smiled at her.

She threw herself at his feet, the flowers flying everywhere. "Lord!" she cried out. "Rabbi! It's you."

"Go tell the others," said the Master. "We have work to do, and it begins today."

Mary ran down the hill on her glad mission. Cherem stayed beside Yeshua. That was his place. Others might come and go, others might fear or love. But the Master's dog knew what he had to do. He had to stay close to Yeshua.

The two of them followed Mary into Jerusalem, where they joined the other followers of Yeshua, all except for the betrayer and the one called Thomas the Doubter. The followers crowded around their Master so closely that Cherem was pushed aside. Since Yeshua was happy to greet his friends again, the dog didn't mind being left out. He sat by the dinner table licking his paws and waiting for someone to toss him some leftovers.

"Mary told us you had come back," Peter said, "but we couldn't believe the good news. I ran all the way to the tomb."

"So did I," said young John. "When we saw the tomb was empty, we came back here to wait for you."

"And where is Thomas?" Yeshua looked around him. "Didn't you tell him to come?"

"Yes," said Peter, "But you know how Thomas is. He said he wouldn't believe you had come back from the grave unless he put his hand in your wounds."

Cherem was shocked at the picture in Peter's mind. If anyone touched such wounds as Yeshua had, it would surely hurt. The Master had been hurt enough, in his opinion, and he growled a little, imagining the scene Thomas had in mind. A good thing for you, Thomas, he thought, that you aren't here. I'd give you a wound of your own to stick your fingers in.

Not long after their reunion, Yeshua met his friends again. This time, Thomas the Doubter was there, looking as guilty, Cherem thought, as a dog that had just eaten the family dinner. Thomas sank down on his knees in front of Yeshua, tears filling his eyes.

"Well, Thomas," Yeshua said, showing Thomas the bloody marks on his body. The marks were still raw, but Cherem was relieved to see that they were healing fast. "Would you like to touch me?"

Thomas broke down and covered his face with his hands. "My Lord and my God," he said.

The doubter didn't have to touch the wounds, Cherem was happy to see, but he watched Thomas carefully. If the man did what he had said he wanted to do, Cherem was prepared to knock him down and sit on him. Maybe even a little nip, he thought, but just then Yeshua looked at him, shaking his head. The dog lay down on the floor and put his paws over his eyes, ashamed.

"You've seen me, Thomas," Yeshua said, "so you believe. Many will believe in me who have not seen this body. And they will be blessed for their faith."

The next day, Yeshua and Cherem left the room before the others woke up. The dog was glad to have his Master all to himself again. They moved through the quiet streets and watched the light of dawn brighten the eastern sky, making the buildings and walls of Jerusalem shine like gold. Hardly anyone was stirring except the guards at the city wall, but these men seemed not to see the Master and his dog pass through the newly-opened gates. Cherem was glad that the soldiers had no idea who they were letting out of Jerusalem. If they had known it was Yeshua, Cherem worried, they might have taken him back to the priests and the Roman ruler.

"Let's head for Emmaus," Yeshua said to Cherem. "The others will find us on the way."

Cherem heeled, walking proudly beside his Master. He had no idea where Emmaus was and didn't care. As long as Yeshua was next to him, life was the way it should be. The dog's head was held high, and he pranced with a lightness in his step he hadn't felt since he was young.

Some of Yeshua's friends came their way and invited the stranger to eat with them. Cherem couldn't understand why the men didn't know they were walking beside the Master, but then Mary of Magdala had not known Yeshua right away, either. The Master was taller, more joyful, more glowing and happy than Cherem had ever seen him. Probably that was because the terrible time of pain and grief was behind him. But his scent was the same, and that was all that the dog needed. Cherem did not understand the idea of "always," but he hoped nothing would ever change again. He wanted to go on walking forever with his Master. That was his idea of heaven.

When Yeshua broke bread with his friends, they suddenly knew who he was and began to cry with joy. Cherem danced around them on his hind legs, glad they knew what he knew. Yeshua was back.

They traveled around for a little while, meeting quietly with friends who had come out of hiding, having heard Yeshua was alive. All of them said they had been afraid to be known as friends of the Master until they understood that death didn't matter. They had been afraid to die for their faith, these people admitted. Yeshua understood why they had hidden in the hills, afraid to confess that they were his disciples. If he had not come back from death, they would have stayed afraid and hidden forever. Now they came out in the open, ready to die as their Master had died. Now, like Cherem, they were no longer afraid.

The dog followed Yeshua and his friends up on a hill. More and more people swelled their numbers. They seemed to know something was about to happen that was new under the sun. Cherem had heard them say earlier that Yeshua might be about to leave them, and the dog's heart beat so hard his chest hurt. Could it really be true that Yeshua was going to leave again, this time for good? Maybe he'll take me with him, the dog thought in a panic. Didn't he promise we would always be together? I'm sure I heard him promise that.

The people were silent and solemn, their eyes on the Master. Except for some birds singing in a fig tree, there was silence. Yeshua stood on the crest of the hill, allowing only Cherem to stay close to him. The Master reached down a last time to touch his dog.

"Now it's time for me to leave you so the Spirit can take my place," he said to his followers. "Go, and tell our people what I have told you. Tell them that compassion for all life is my message. Go, and tell the world that God loves his creation, that God blesses all the life in it, all the suffering and joy that comes with living. I will be with you always."

Cherem pressed close against Yeshua's leg and whimpered a little. He wanted to say good-by, since their earthly time was at an end, but didn't want to cry. Cherem hoped he was too old and wise a dog for that.

"It's all right, Cherem," Yeshua said, his arms wide in blessing. "Wait for me here. I will not forget you."

There was a sudden flash of light, like the one that Cherem had seen in the stone tomb, before Yeshua had waked from his long sleep. For a few minutes, no one could see anything. Some people rubbed their eyes as if they hurt from the brightness. Yeshua was no longer there. Everyone looked around for him, then up in the air, mouths open in surprise.

After a while, the people went away, talking in whispers about the work they needed to do for the

Master. The dog understood why they left. Yeshua was gone, and there was nothing more to see. Cherem wondered if he should go with them, but his heart told him to stay where Yeshua had last been. Others would spread the good news. Cherem had his own work to do. It was to be still and wait.

Through days of rain and cold, the dog remained alone on the hilltop. He drank a little water when it rained, but had no nourishment except the memory of his Master's touch. Cherem lay exactly where Yeshua had stood before the light took him away. The old dog grew thinner over the days and weeks, but did not leave.

What if Yeshua came back, he thought, and didn't find his dog? Cherem could not risk that happening. He would stay exactly where the Master had told him to stay. When one of the Marys came to feed him and tried to coax him to go home with her, Cherem refused to eat or move.

One night his eyes became dim and his heartbeat slower. He knew that his time on earth was short, and he was glad. In the moments before he died, Cherem saw his Master come toward him, surrounded by light. It looked as if the heavens had been torn open and stars were pouring through the hole in the sky, spinning like pinwheels around the shining figure of his Master.

Yeshua smiled and reached out to him in welcome. The dog felt young again, and he leaped up into the arms that would hold him forever. Cherem took his last breath and was home.

MOON BLUE

The poignant story of a battle-fatigued WW II hero's homecoming.

Sgt. Rollins is a young white southerner with a Medal of Honor in his pocket, a load of shrapnel in his back, and a mission to find the missing granddaughter of the Black woman who raised him. Before solving a murder case, he falls in love and finds himself in more danger than on the battlefield of Guadalcanal.

$9.95 U.S.
$10.95 Canada
078-0-9834956-1-1

 SpiritBooks